The Prince Protects His People

Amy Lykosh

Sonlight Curriculum, Ltd.
8042 South Grant Way
Littleton, CO 80122-2705
USA

sonlight.com
main@sonlight.com
(303) 730-6292

ISBN 978-1-935570-89-9
Printed in the United States of America

The Prince Protects His People

Amy Lykosh

To Jadon,
"God has heard,"
one of the wall-builders
Nehemiah's listed

Preface

Why Nehemiah?

David strides through the pages of the Old Testament as a larger-than-life character. The high king, the greatest poet, the most successful general, the man after God's own heart. He's like a combination of Richard the Lionhearted, Shakespeare, Alexander the Great, and Mother Teresa.

Which is both amazing . . . and completely unrelatable.

Nehemiah comes to us on a more human scale.

Sort of.

Nehemiah the Man

Like Daniel before him, Nehemiah served in the court of the king. Both of them were probably eunuchs. Both were highly trusted and deeply trustworthy. Both maintained some level of influence with leaders from different empires. Both must have been incredibly charismatic and tremendously good at the game of politics.

Both were tremendously zealous for the Law of God.

But while Daniel wrote prophecies, Nehemiah wrote histories.

Nehemiah, as cupbearer, was the king's trusted confidant. When Nehemiah asks to be excused from his duties for a time, the king plaintively asks, "How soon will you return?" He would miss his friend.

Nehemiah must have been an incredibly competent administrator, setting up systems to make sure goods, materials, and people were where they needed to be, all while keeping meticulous records.

He was, as you will see, not motivated by gain. Can you imagine a public official today refusing his pay? Nehemiah did.

You might say that he's one of the best examples of a white-collar worker in the Bible. Though he was never officially a CEO of a company, he headed an enormous public works project he had planned, then served as governor for twelve years.

I love that the Bible offers the story of a man who would have loved spreadsheets, along with the stories of those more dramatic kings and conquerors.

So: cupbearer, politician, trusted confidant, 12-year governor, administrator, world-class historian, strong leader, treasured employee, successful fund-raiser, altruist, even a prince . . . clearly a man of tremendous giftedness.

So much of what he records is matter-of-fact, "And then I did this and made that happen."

He strides about like the ruler he is.

But then there are short, almost forlorn prayers: "Remember me, O Lord."

He was, after all, human.

A Man of the Mundane

A friend once said, "Life is maintenance."

And it's so true. Do the dishes. Mow the grass. Change the oil. Eat. Sleep.

This is one of my favorite parts of the story of Nehemiah. He was the cup-bearer to the king. Then he had a dramatic, high-point in life project. And the people had a dramatic return to God.

But after that, he had to keep doing maintenance, to keep correcting the people. Though the men finished the wall in two months, Nehemiah spent his entire time as governor focused on continuing to maintain and repair it.

This is so terribly human, so real. It's like the story of Cinderella continues after the wedding, when she and Prince Charming have to deal with emotions and health issues, with unhelpful staff and sometimes disobedient children.

That's not as fun a story, though it is more realistic.

Nehemiah finished his major triumph in the first few chapters of his book, and then has to keep going. What a beautiful, honest picture of life.

Nehemiah the Historian

In the Bible, the book of Nehemiah includes a lot of names. I think, as a historian, it was the equivalent of including all the signatures on the Declaration of Independence. Most of us just read the text of the Declaration, especially the famous second paragraph: "We hold these truths to be self-evident, that all men are created equal, that they are endowed by their Creator with certain unalienable Rights, that among these are Life, Liberty and the pursuit of Happiness."

We skip the 56 signatures at the end.

But to a historian, those 56 names mean something. Each name has his own story, too.

I think something like that comes into play with Nehemiah.

A Man of Prayer

Years ago, my mom mentioned a fact she had learned in Bible study: Nehemiah prayed for four months, and then built the wall in only two.

I had never noticed that. He calls the months by the Jewish calendar names, not the month names given by the Romans some centuries later. And the Jewish calendar doesn't exactly line up with the Western calendar.

So when Nehemiah says Chisleu, he means sometime in our November or December. Nisan is sometime in March or April.

Such a great story! But how easy to miss!

When you read through Nehemiah's story, he is constantly praying:

- Four months of earnest intercession for all the people: "Grant me mercy in the sight of my master."

- Prayers of protection for beloved Jerusalem against the enemy: "Hear, O our God, for we are despised."

- Corporate prayers before work: "We made our prayer unto our God. Then set a watch against them day and night."

- Prayers for personal steadfastness in the face of malice: "Now therefore, O God, strengthen my hands."

- Prayers for justice: "Remember the works" of those who stood against him.

- Plaintive pleas that God has been paying attention to his specific actions: "Think upon me, my God, for good."

And his prayers sound so normal! No unusual words or images that need additional explanation.

Just simple statements that you or I might make, said throughout his life.

May it be so for you and me, too.

A Note on This Style

I am not a patient person, and I tend to be a stickler for accurate facts. So I don't like it when I read biographies that include lines like, "He tossed his scarf over his shoulder and went out the door."

How did the author know the man wore a scarf?! And even if he did, what if the man waited until he got out the door to toss his scarf?

With the rise of the novel-in-verse, the method of story-telling has shifted. The story flows quickly, has no extra, unnecessary details, and penetrates to the emotions.

This is a biography-in-verse. I tried to avoid made-up details and get to the essence. Starting with the King James Version as a base, I worked through the book of Nehemiah verse by verse, trying to make the story as clear as possible.

My goal has been to retain Nehemiah's voice, but also answer my own questions about the events.

Amy Lykosh
Esmont, VA
    • 27 May 2019

Prologue

Before

In the time of Moses,
The people made a covenant with God.

They didn't keep it.

God was, according to his name,
Merciful and gracious,
Slow to anger despite constant insults,
Abundant in goodness and truth.
He showed mercy to thousands,
Forgiving iniquity and transgression and sin ...

And yet the people rejected him,
Turned to idols,
Ignored his laws.

In time, the chosen people

Divided.

The northern tribes of Israel,
With Judah to the south.
Enemies.

The Assyrians came first.
They took the ten tribes of Israel.

Then the Babylonians came,
And Judah fell.
Tens of thousands of Jews
Went into captivity.

God's people
Evicted
From the promised land.

Seek the Peace

As the Lord of hosts commanded,
In Babylon the people
Built houses to live in;
Planted gardens and ate of the fruit.
They married and were given in marriage,
Had children and grandchildren.

As in the time of the Israelites in Egypt,
They increased and were not diminished.

The God of Israel said to
Seek the peace of the city
And pray to the Lord for it,

For peace in the city meant
Peace for the dwellers of the city,
Both those voluntary and those forced.

And they waited for the seventy years to end,
When God would cause the people to return
To Jerusalem,

The City of Peace.

Waiting

The Lord said:

"I know the thoughts that I think toward you:
Thoughts of peace, and not of evil,
To give you an expected end.

Then shall you call upon me,
And go and pray unto me,
And I will listen to you.

And you shall seek me,
And find me,
When you shall search for me with all your heart.

And I will be found of you:
And I will turn away your captivity,
And I will gather you from all the nations,
And from all the places where I have driven you.

And I will bring you again
Into the place where you had been
Carried away
Captive."

In Babylon News

454 B.C.
It was the ninth month
When Hanani reached Shusan,
Where I served in the palace.

I asked him:
"Those Jews who escaped exile and remained in the land—
How are they?
And how is Jerusalem?"

The news—far worse than I had thought.

"Those who remain are in great trouble
And disgrace.
The walls are destroyed,
And the gates, burned."

Without a Wall

No wall? This means
> Living in fear.
> No protection.
> Subject to the whims of any passing enemy.

Response

I sat and wept
      And mourned
      And fasted
      And prayed.

Prayer

O Lord God of heaven,
The great and terrible God,
That keeps covenant and mercy
For them that love him
And observe his commandments:

Listen to me now.
Open your eyes!
Hear the prayer of your servant!
I'm praying this, day and night,
On behalf of the children of Israel.

We have sinned against you:
I, and my father's house.
We have not kept the commands,
       Nor the decrees,
       Nor the laws,
Which you commanded.

You told Moses that if we transgress,
You would scatter us abroad among the nations.
Clearly, you keep your word.

But . . .

If we turn to you, and keep your commandments,
Even if we were cast out
Unto the uttermost part of the heaven,
Yet will you gather us again,
And bring us to the place
Where you have chosen to set your name.

Now these are your servants and your people,
Whom you have redeemed by your great power,
And by your strong hand.
Keep your word again!
O Lord, I beseech you,

Listen to the prayer of your servant,
And to the prayers of your servants,
Who desire to fear your name.
Prosper your servant this day . . .

And grant me mercy
In the sight of my master.

Four Months

Four months I prayed,
With those who also feared the Lord.

Four months of working
With no hint of my pain,

Four months of deep grief,
Waiting for the next step.

Four months
I planned and I prayed.

My Work

I was the king's cupbearer,
His friend and trusted confidant.

In the presence of the king
I observed statesmanship,

As the king led
The nation.

Request

In the first month of the new year,
As was my responsibility,
I brought wine to the great king.

Until that day, I had shown no sign of sorrow.

But now the king noticed, and asked,
"Why do you look so sad?
You aren't sick.
Are you heart-sick?"

In Fear

Then I was terrified.
Downcast spirits were not permitted in the king's presence,
And I could be destroyed.
Nevertheless, I replied,

"Let the king live for ever.
Why should not my face be sad?
The city with my fathers' graves lies in waste;
The gates, burned."

Promise of Help

The king replied,
"What would you like me to do?"

Again, I prayed to the God of heaven.

Then I said to the king,
"Please. If I have found favor in your sight,
Send me to Judah, to the city of my fathers' tombs,
That I may build it."

The king, Queen Esther at his side, asked,
"How long will it take you to get there?
When will you return?"

The seed of my prayers and planning
Now sprouted.

I gave him not only a time estimate,
But asked for specific needs.

How to Help

I need letters to the governors beyond the river,
That they may transport me safely until I come into my homeland.

Also a letter to Asaph, the keeper of the king's forest.
May he give me timber to make beams
      For the gates of the fortress by the palace,
      For the wall of the city,
      For the house where I shall live.

The king gave me all I asked for,
Because the good hand of God was upon me.

In one day I went
From weeping servant
To well-provisioned director of public works.

In Retrospect

For the king to notice
With Esther the Jew at his side . . .
Could his question have come
At a better time?

In Jerusalem

The Trip

When I came to the governors beyond the river,
I gave them the king's letters.

We had no trouble on the trip.
The king had sent captains of the army and horsemen with me.

The Enemy

Now hear of the two who took note of my coming
Without gladness:

By name, Sanballat the Moabite,
And Tobiah the Ammonite.

The Moabites were descended of Lot and his elder daughter,
And worshipped Chemosh;

The Ammonites were descended of Lot and his younger daughter,
And worshipped Molech.

When they learned that a man had come
To seek the good of the children of Israel,

They were greatly displeased,
Though not yet threatened.

I was, after all, but one man
With few companions,

Surrounded by enemies,
Among the afflicted in Jerusalem.

In Stealth

After I was three days in Jerusalem,
I rose in the night
In secret
With a few men.

I had told no man
What God had put in my heart to do at Jerusalem.

I rode out by night
And viewed the walls of Jerusalem,
Which were broken down,
And the gates,
Consumed with fire.

By the gate of the valley,
Before the dragon well,
To the dung port,
And on to the gate of the fountain,
And to the king's pool.
There, my beast could not go forward . . .
The ruin was too great.

So I went up in the night by the brook,
That rain-fed torrent then low enough that I could travel,
And viewed the wall.

Then I turned back,
And entered again by the gate of the valley.

The rulers knew nothing of my stealthy surveillance.

Exhortation

I had told my plan, thus far, to
       Neither Jews,
       Nor priests,
       Nor nobles,
       Nor rulers (those Babylonian magistrates),
       Nor the rest that did the work.

But then I said to them,
"You see the distress that we are in,
How Jerusalem lies in waste,
And the gates are burned with fire.

Come.

Let us build up the wall of Jerusalem,
That we be no more a disgrace.

The hand of my God is good upon me,
And I have the backing of the great king."

Rise Up

And they said,
"Let us rise up and build."

So they strengthened their hands for this good work.

First Reaction

Then Sanballat and Tobiah,
With Geshem the Arabian,

Laughed us to scorn,
And despised us.

"What is this thing that you do?
Will you rebel against the great king?"

Response

Surrounded by rubble,
Mocked by the enemy—

Hardly a glorious beginning.

Yet I had come this far already.
And so I said,

"The God of heaven,
He will prosper us.

Therefore, we his servants will
Arise and build.

But you have no share,
Nor legal right,

Nor memorial,
In Jerusalem."

Building

Gates

A city has no safety without a wall.

The gates, those places of entry and exit,
The most obvious points of attack, and thus
Vital to the protection of the city.

Say their names with proper honor.

The Sheep Gate.
The Fish Gate.
The Old Gate.
The Valley Gate.
The Dung Gate.
The Gate of the Fountain.
The Water Gate.
The Horse Gate.
The East Gate.
The Gate of Registry.

Gates Restored

Faithful men laid the beams,
      And set up the doors,
      And the locks,
      And the bars.

Names

All the names of the men,
And the portions of the walls and gates they rebuilt—
I recorded all.
Faithful men
Who caught the vision,
Rose up,
And worked.

And among the names is Shallum . . .

And his daughters.

The contribution of these women
Is both recorded
And remembered.

Not That Easy

The workers faithfully worked.
Sanballat heard that
Despite his taunts,
We built the wall.
He flew into a rage.
He mocked the Jews
Before his comrades
And the Samaritan army.

The Samaritans:
Those Israelites in former days,
Who created their own Temple,
On their own Temple mountain,
A rival place of worship.

None of them rejoiced to hear how
The chosen people rise up.

Sanballat spoke to the Samaritans.
"What are these weak Jews working on?
Do they think they'll be able to protect themselves?
Will they restore their Temple?
Will they finish in a day?
Will they recover the stones from the rubbish piles?"

Then Tobiah took up the taunt.
"The wall they're building is so weak,
That even a fox, walking lightly,
Would break down their wall.
Pathetic fortification!"

Prayer

Hear, O our God;
For we are despised,

And turn their insults back on their own heads,
And let them be taken as plunder to the land of captivity.

Do not cover their guilt,
Or blot out their sins from your sight,

For they have provoked you to anger
In the presence of the builders.

Halfway

Despite the taunts, we kept raising the wall.

The people had a mind to work,
And all the wall was joined together,
And rose to half its height.

It took less time than you would expect.

Conspiracy

When Sanballat,
> And Tobiah,
> And the Arabians,
> And the Ammonites,
> And the Ashdodites (sometimes called Philistines),

When all these heard that the walls of Jerusalem were rising,
And that the breaches began to be repaired,
They were very angry.

They conspired, all of them together,
To come and to fight against Jerusalem,
And to hinder the wall-building.

While we were seeking to birth a new protection,
They were hoping to cause a miscarriage.

On Guard

We made our prayer unto our God.

Then set a watch against them day and night.

Falling Apart

Then my people said,
"Our strength is decaying, trying to haul materials.
There is too much rubbish—piles and heaps.
We are not able to build the wall."

And our enemies said,
"They shall have no advance warning.
No matter what guards they set in place,
They shall not see
Till we suddenly come in the midst of them,
And kill them,
And cause the work to cease."

And the Jews who lived next door to the Samaritans came,
And ten times they said,
"No matter where you go,
They will attack and defeat you."

Leadership

When all falls apart,
The leader must renew the vision,
        Must increase defenses,
        Must encourage and inspire.

If I looked to the past,
My skillset included
Not dying from poison.

But I had been in the presence of the great king.
I had all I needed to fulfill the vision.

Response

Not only did we have watchmen.
Now I set up a defense system.
The people, according to their families,
Prepared with their swords,
      Their spears,
      Their bows.

Should an enemy approach,
We would be ready to fight.

And I looked, and rose up,
And said unto the nobles,
      And to the rulers,
      And to the rest of the people:

"Be not afraid of them!
Remember the Lord,
Which is great and terrible,

And fight
      For your brethren,
      Your sons,
      Your daughters,
      Your wives,
      Your houses!"

No Great Threat

Our enemies heard
That we knew their secret plans,
That God had brought their schemes to

Nothing.

That we returned,
All of us,
To the wall,
Every one to his work.

Half and Half

Half worked.

The other half
      Held spears
      Held shields
      Held bows
      Held armor.

The princes encouraged and helped
All the house of Judah.

Prudence

The workers—
Those who built the wall,
And those who carried supplies,—
All had one hand to work
And one hand ready to weapon.

Swords at our sides,
We built.

The Plan

The trumpeter stayed near me,
Ready to sound the alarm.

Then I said to the people,
"The work is great and large,

And we are separated as we work upon the wall,
One far from another.

Wherever and whenever you hear
The sound of the trumpet,

Go there quickly:
Our God shall fight for us.

And let everyone, with his servant,
Stay here in Jerusalem.

In the night,
Together we make an adequate guard,

And in the day,
We are ready to work."

In community
There is safety.

Focus

Our plans laid,
Our preparations made,
We labored in the work.

And half of them held the spears
From the rising of the morning
Till the stars appeared.

And neither I,
  Nor my brethren,
  Nor my servants,
  Nor the Persian men of the guard which followed me,
None of us ever undressed, even for bed.
We went with our tools or our weapons.
No break in focus, even when we drew water.

Setback

Shocking

Then the common people,
Both men and women,
Gave a great cry
Against their Jewish brothers.

"We, our sons, and our daughters, are many,
And our large families need large amounts of food,
That we may eat, and live.

We have had famine,
And in order to buy food,
We have mortgaged our lands,
      Our vineyards,
      Our houses."

And others said,
"The king's tax has been heavy.
We borrowed money
Upon our lands and vineyards."

And the common people gave a great cry and said,
"We are Jews, and our brothers are Jews.
Our children are like their children.

Yet our sons and daughters
Are servants and slaves,
Forced into a lifetime of bondage.

And since other men now hold
Our lands and our vineyards,
We have no power to redeem our children."

Worse Than I Thought

Hanani had not mentioned this.
"Great trouble and disgrace"—
Yes.
"Walls torn down and gates, burned"—
Yes.

But the deliberate enslavement of one's brothers?
Offering not help for the hurting,
But seeing instead a get-rich-quick scheme?

I was very angry when I heard the cry of the common people.

The Law

God's commandment,
Given through Moses,
Was clear:

"You shall not deduct interest
From loans to your kinsman,
Whether in money or food or anything else.

You may deduct interest
From loans to foreigners,
But do not deduct interest
From loans to your countrymen,

So that Yahweh your God
May bless you in all your undertakings
In the land that you are about to enter and possess. "

And the Prophets

David asked,
"Lord, who shall abide in thy tabernacle?
Who shall dwell in thy holy hill?"

One of his answers:
"He that does not charge interest,
Nor takes reward against the innocent.

He that acts rightly
Shall never be moved. "

Or take this Proverb:
"Whoever increases wealth
By taking interest or profit from the poor
Grows the wealth for someone else,
Who will be kind to the poor. "

Self-Destruct

These people live in a ruined land,
A daily reminder
That those who disobey,
God punishes.

Yet these nobles and officials behave
Against all reason and uprightness,
Ignoring the command,
Looking out for themselves.

If they truly wanted to act
In their own self-interest,
They should be obedient.
They they would never be moved.

Charged

I rebuked the nobles and officials,
And charged them:
"You lend your own people money
And charge interest! "

Public Meeting

I held an assembly and said,
"Nobles and officials!
We are doing all we can
To buy back—to redeem!—
Our Jewish brothers,
Sold to the nations.
Then you sell them again?
And so we have to buy them back again?
How many times must we redeem them?"

The nobles said nothing.
What could they say?
I continued.

"This is no good.
You should walk
In the fear of our God.
Instead, our enemies taunt us,
And we dwell in disgrace and shame,
Our promised land a ruin.

My helpers and I have been
Lending money and food,
As needed.
But as the Law commands,
We don't charge interest.

Stop it already!

Restore, I pray you, to them,
Even this day,
  Their lands,
  Their vineyards,
  Their olive yards,
  Their houses.

Restore also the interest they've paid you
  For money,
  And food,
  And wine,
  And oil."

Transformed

The nobles said,
"We will restore them,
And will require nothing of the people.
We will do as you say."

So I called the priests,
And made the nobles and officials
Take an oath
That they should do what they said.

Then I shook out the folds of my robe.
"So may God shake out every man
      From his house,
      And from his labor,
That does not keep this promise.
Even thus may he be shaken out, and
Emptied."

And all the assembly said,
"Amen!"
And praised the LORD.

And the people did according to this promise.

Pushback

No Breach

By now the wall had no breach,
Though the gates were not yet in place.

And Sanballat, Tobiah, and Geshem,
And the rest of our enemies,
Sent to me, saying,

"Come, let us meet together
In one of the villages
In the plain of Ono."

Such an obvious plot
For treachery and murder.

By Messenger

"I am doing a great work,
So that I cannot come down.

Why should the work cease,
While I travel twenty miles to you?"

Stratagem

Four times they wrote to me
With similar requests.

Four times I wrote back
With similar responses.

The fifth time, Sanballat his servant
Brought an unsealed envelope,

So any who had wished to read it
Was given opportunity.

Here was a new trick.
Sanballat wrote,

"Geshem and the heathen report
That you and the Jews think to rebel.

That's why you're building the wall,
So you, Nehemiah, may be king.

I also hear that you appointed prophets
To preach in Jerusalem, saying,

'There is a king in Judah.'
I shall report all of this to the great king.

But before I do,
Come now, and let us meet together."

The plan, of course,
Was to make us afraid,

For if we lived in fear,
Our hands would be weakened from the work.

And the wall would not be done.

By Messenger

"There are no such things done as you say.
You've made up this story
Out of your own heart."

Prayer

Now therefore, O God,
Strengthen my hands.

In Cahoots

After this, I came to the house of Shemaiah.
He said, "Let us meet together
In the house of God, within the Temple.
And let us shut the doors of the Temple,
For they will come to slay you—
Truly, in the night they will come to slay you."

And I said, "Should such a man as I flee?
Am I a coward?
What kind of example would that set for the people?

And beyond that, what governor would go into the Temple to save
his life?
God gave the altar and the priest's office
To the sons of Aaron.
Remember the story of Uzziah,
King of Judah,
Who went into the Temple to burn incense
And was struck with leprosy until his dying day?
I will not go in."

He recommended a course of action
Against the law of God,
So I recognized that God had not sent him,
But that he pronounced this prophecy against me
Because Tobiah and Sanballat had hired him
To make me afraid, and go into the Temple, and sin.

See the evil scheme they devised:
Even if God did not strike me down
For disobedience,
I would have shown cowardice before the people,
And Sanballat and Tobiah would have an evil report,
That they might discredit me.

Tobiah

Tobiah was married to a Jewish woman
And his son was married to the daughter of one of the builders of
wall.

Some of the nobles sent letters to Tobiah,
And he sent letters back.

And they reported his good deeds before me,
And uttered my words to him.

There were many in Judah sworn unto him.
And Tobiah sent letters to put me in fear.

I was not the leader of
A single-minded movement of enthusiasts.

Prayer

"My God, remember the works
Of Tobiah and Sanballat,

And on the prophetess Noadiah,
And the rest of the prophets,
That would have put me in fear."

This is not a prayer of forgiveness.
This is a prayer of honesty.

Finished

Despite all this,
The wall was finished in fifty and two days.

The materials were there (though broken down).
The hand of God was upon us to help.

I had prayed four months
Before I acted.

Once there, less than two months
To complete the wall.

More prayer time
Than work time.

It is something to note.

Cast Down

When all our enemies heard of the completion of the wall,
And all the heathen saw these things,
They were disheartened,
For they realized that this work was accomplished
With the help of our God.

Maintenance

When the wall was built,
And the doors were put in their place,
And the gatekeepers
      And the singers
      And the Levites
Were put in charge,

Then I gave the responsibility
Of ruling Jerusalem
To two trustworthy men.

To Hanani,
The original message-bearer,
And to Hananiah,
The commander of the fortress.

This commander was truth's own man,
And though answerable to the great king,
He revered God more than most.

Instructions

I said to Hanani and Hananiah,

"No need to open the gates at sunrise.
Wait until the sun is hot to open the gates—
It's takes less manpower to guard a closed door.
Let those on guard close and bar the doors.

Appoint the residents of Jerusalem as guards,
Each to his own watch,
Some as sentries at a post,
And some as guards near their homes."

At That Time

Jerusalem was open,
And great,

But there were few people,
And the houses were not yet rebuilt.

At this time, I returned to Babylon.

Back to Jerusalem

Interlude

426 B.C.
Twenty-eight years pass.
The great king went to rest with his fathers,

And a new great king took his place,
Until he, too, went to rest with his fathers.

The Babylonian empire fell,
And the Persian empire ascended.

Ezra went to Jerusalem
With tens of thousands of men.

This is where my story
Resumes.

Genealogy

In Jerusalem again, my God put into my heart
To assemble the nobles,
      And the rulers,
      And the people,
That they might be registered by genealogy,
A record of those who first returned to the land,
The names of the Jewish exiles
Who returned from captivity.

Though Nebuchadnezzar, king of Babylon,
Had carried them away,
They came again to Jerusalem and to Judah,
Every one to his city.

The record begins
with Zerubbabel,
The governor;
Next his helper Joshua,
Whose name means
"Yahweh is salvation."

Then myself
And all the rest,
Our names preserved.

The smallest family to register,
The men of Bethazmaveth,
Had just forty and two.
The largest family,
The children of Senaah,
Had three thousand nine hundred and thirty.

Also descendants of the Gibeonites,
Those who had recognized the true God
And, by trickery, preserved their lives
In the time of Joshua,
Grafted in now to the rise and fall
Of the children of Israel.
Called Nethinim, they served the Temple.

Among those who returned:
      973 priests,
      74 Levites,
      148 singers, those children of Asaph,
      138 gatekeepers,
      392 Nethinim, Temple servants.

Unknown Origin

Some who went up
Could not prove their ancestry,
The records lost or corrupted.

I said to them that
They should not eat of the most holy things,
Till a priest could inquire of the Lord on their behalf.

Total

The whole congregation together
Was forty and two thousand three hundred and threescore.

There were also servants and singers,
Horses, mules, camels, donkeys.

Temple, Rebuilding

With a return of the people,
It was time for the Temple
To be rebuilt.

Some of the chiefs of the fathers gave to the work:
     Gold,
     Ceremonial bowls,
     Silver,
     Priestly garments.

City Dwelling

So the priests,
      And the Levites,
      And the gatekeepers,
      And the singers,
      And some of the people,
      And the Nethinim,
      And all Israel,
Dwelt in their cities.

And when the seventh month came,
The children of Israel were in their cities.

Every Seven Years

Moses, in his final address to the people,
Gave this charge:

"At the end of every seven years,
In the solemnity of the year of release from all debts,
During the feast of tabernacles,

When all Israel is come to appear
Before the Lord your God
In the place which he shall choose,

You shall read this law
Before all Israel
In their hearing.

Gather the people together,
Men and women, and children,
And the stranger that is within your gates,

That they may hear,
And that they may learn,
And fear the Lord your God,

And observe to do all the words of this law:
And that their children,
Which have not known any thing,

May hear,
And learn to fear the Lord your God,
As long as you live in the land which you go over Jordan to possess. "

Remind Us

It was the seventh month,
During the feast of tabernacles,
And all the people
Gathered themselves together as one man
Into the square before the Water Gate.

They told Ezra the scribe
To bring out the book of the law of Moses,
Which the Lord had commanded to Israel.

Reading

And Ezra the priest
Brought the law
Before the congregation
Both of men and women,
And all that could hear with understanding,
On the first day of the seventh month.

And he faced the square before the Water Gate
And read from early morning until midday,
Before the men and the women,
And those that could understand.
And the ears of all the people
Were attentive to the book of the law.

Witness This Now

Ezra the scribe stood on a wooden platform,
Made specifically for this purpose.

To his right stood six priests,
And to his left stood seven.

Fourteen priests in all,
Seven doubled, seven intensified.

Seven, the number of spiritual perfection,
The hallmark of the work of God's spirit.

See the miracle of the reading
This day, in the sight of all the people.

At the Start

All the people saw Ezra,
Standing on the platform above them.
And when he opened the book,
All the people stood up.

And Ezra blessed the Lord, the great God.
And all the people answered, "Amen, Amen,"
And lifted up their hands.
Then they bowed their heads,
And worshipped the Lord
With their faces to the ground.

A Lengthy Sermon

Ezra read,
And the Levites explained the law
While the people stayed in their places.

So they read in the book in the law of God,
Distinctly and clearly, so that all could hear.

And they explained the meaning,
Translating as needed, from the Hebrew into Aramaic.

They made sure that the people understood,
Point by point.

Conviction

All the people wept,
When they heard the words of the law.

Correction

Then I, Nehemiah,
And Ezra, the priest, the scribe,
And the Levites that taught the people

Said to all the people,
"This day is holy to the Lord your God;
Mourn not, nor weep."

And I said,
"Go your way,
Eat rich food,

And drink sweet wine,
And send portions to those
Who didn't prepare.

For this day is holy to our Lord.
Do not grieve,
For the joy of the Lord is your strength."

Backwards

It may not be what you'd expect—
To tell the people to stop grieving
And start celebrating

At the moment they first understood
What the Lord requires.
Backwards, perhaps . . . but commanded.

Celebrate

So the Levites stilled all the people,
Saying, "Hold your peace,
For the day is holy;
Neither grieve."

And all the people went their way
        To eat,
        And to drink,
        And to share their food,
        And to celebrate with great joy,
Because they had understood
The words that were declared to them.

The Second Day

On the second day,
The heads of the families of all the people,
> The priests,
> And the Levites,
Gathered again with Ezra the scribe,
To understand the words of the law.

And they found written in the law
Which the Lord had commanded through Moses,
That the children of Israel
Should dwell in booths
In the feast of the seventh month,

And that they should proclaim it
And spread the news in all their cities,
And in Jerusalem, saying,
"Go to the hill country,
And fetch branches of
> Olive,
> Pine,
> Myrtle,
> Palm,
> And other leafy trees,
To make booths,
As it is written."

Feast of Booths

When the children of Israel
Left Egypt,
They dwelt in the wilderness
Forty years.

The Lord commanded that
For seven days each year,
They make booths
And live in them,

That the generations to come
Would know
That God the Lord brought them
Out of the land of bondage.

Building

So the people went out,
And brought back branches,
And made themselves booths,
    On their roofs
    In their courtyards,
    In the courtyard of the house of God,
    In the square by the Water Gate,
    In the square by the Gate of Ephraim.

First Time

The whole company that returned
From captivity
Made booths and lived in them.

From the days of Joshua, son of Nun,
To that very day,
The children of Israel had not done so.

And there was very great gladness.
They, too, had been brought
Out of the land of bondage.

More

From the building of a wall
To the building of a booth—

A prayer began a transformation
Of more than just a city's walls:

The hearts of the people change,
A new celebration in the Promised Land.

The Whole Feast

Day by day,
From the first day
To the last day,

Ezra read in the book of the law of God.

And they kept the feast seven days.
And on the eighth day was a solemn assembly,
As the Law instructed.

Foundation

It was after this celebration
That the foundation of the Temple
Was again laid.

As Ezra recorded,
"All the people shouted with a great shout,
When they praised the Lord,
Because the foundation of the house of the Lord
Was laid.

But many of the priests
     And Levites
     And heads of the households,
Who were ancient men,
That had seen the first Temple,
When the foundation of the second Temple
Was laid before their eyes,
Wept with a loud voice,
And many shouted aloud for joy.

The people could not discern
The noise of the shout of joy
From the noise of the weeping of the people,
For the people shouted with a loud shout,
And the noise was heard afar off."

And again I returned to Babylon.

Governorship

Interlude

419 B.C.
Seven more years pass.

Then I was appointed governor of the land of Judah,
And served in that office for twelve years.

In all that time, neither I nor my assistants
Took the food allowance of the governor.

The former governors had put heavy burdens on the people,
Had taken not only the food allowance of bread and wine,
But added forty shekels of silver as additional tax.
Even their servants lorded it over the people.

But I did not do so, out of the fear of God.

I did not tax the people,
Though 150 Jews and rulers,
Plus visitors from surrounding lands,
Ate at my table.

Daily, the cooks prepared for me
One ox and six choice sheep,
Also poultry.
And once in ten days, all sorts of wine.

Yet for all this, I did not tax the people,
Because the bondage was heavy upon this people.

Daily Life in Jerusalem

I bought no land, but
I continued in the work of this wall,
Maintaining and repairing it,
With the help of my servants.

Think upon me, my God,
For good,
According to all that I have done for this people.

Prophecy

410 B.C.
During my tenure as governor,
The word of the Lord came again

To Haggai,
To correct the people:

"Is it time for you to dwell in paneled houses,
While the house of God continues desolate?

Consider your ways:
>   You have sown much, and bring in little;
>   You eat, but you have not enough;
>   You drink, but you are not satisfied;
>   You clothe yourself, but the clothes do not warm you;
>   You earn wages, but put them in a bag with holes.

Consider your ways:
>   Go to the hills,
>   Bring timber,
>   And build my house,
So I may take pleasure in it and be glorified. "

During my tenure as governor,
The word of the Lord came again

To Haggai,
To comfort the people:

"For thus saith the Lord of hosts:
Yet once more, in a little while,

I will shake the heavens,
    And the earth,
    And the sea,
    And the dry land;

And I will shake all nations,
And the desire of all nations shall come,
And I will fill this house with glory, saith the Lord of hosts.

The glory of this latter house
Shall be greater than of the former,
Saith the Lord of hosts.

And in this place will I give peace. "

Prophecy Again

And the word of the Lord came again,
Only a few months later,

To Zechariah,
That man of dreams and visions.

"Thus saith the Lord of hosts:
I am returned unto Zion,
And will dwell in the midst of Jerusalem:
And Jerusalem shall be called a city of truth,
And the mountain of the Lord of hosts the holy mountain.

Thus saith the Lord of hosts:
Behold, I will save my people from the east country,
And from the west country;
And I will bring them,
And they shall dwell in the midst of Jerusalem.
And they shall be my people,
And I will be their God,
In truth and in righteousness.

Thus saith the Lord of hosts:
For before these days there was no peace to him that went out
Or came in because of the affliction:
For I set all men every one against his neighbor.
But now I will not be unto the residue of this people
As in the former days, saith the Lord of hosts.

For the seed shall be prosperous;
The vine shall give her fruit,
The ground shall give her increase,
And the heavens shall give their dew.
And I will cause the remnant of this people
To possess all these things.

For thus saith the Lord of hosts:
As I thought to punish you,
When your fathers provoked me to wrath,
And I repented not:

So again have I thought in these days
To do well unto Jerusalem
And to the house of Judah.
Fear ye not.

And the word of the Lord of hosts came unto me, saying,
Thus saith the Lord of hosts:
It shall yet come to pass,
That there shall come people,
And the inhabitants of many cities,

And the inhabitants of one city shall go to another, saying,
"Let us go speedily to pray before the Lord,
And to seek the Lord of hosts; I will go also."

Indeed, many people and strong nations
Shall come to seek the Lord of hosts in Jerusalem,
And to pray before the Lord.

Thus saith the Lord of hosts:
In those days it shall come to pass,
That ten men out of all languages of the nations,
Shall take hold of him that is a Jew, saying,
"We will go with you,

For we have heard that God is with you."

End of My Tenure

407 B.C.
When my time as governor was at an end,
The Temple was not yet finished.

The work continued forward,
And I returned to Babylon,

Resuming my duties for the great king.
Under Ezra, the Temple was dedicated.

Later, I earnestly requested leave,
Until I was allowed to return again to Jerusalem.

Another Celebration

On the Twenty-Fourth

404 B.C.
On the twenty-fourth day of the seventh month,
The children of Israel gathered in grief,
> Fasting,
> Wearing prickly sackcloth,
> Purposefully covered in dust.

And the sons of Israel separated themselves
From all foreigners.

The Israelites stood and confessed
> Their sins,
> And the iniquities of their fathers.

And they stood up in their place,
And read in the book of the law of the Lord their God
> One fourth part of the day;
> And another fourth part
> > They confessed,
> > And worshipped the Lord their God.

Then Levites stood upon the platform,
And cried with a loud voice unto the Lord their God.

Doxology

Stand up and bless the Lord your God
For ever and ever.

Blessed be your glorious name,
Which is exalted above all blessing and praise.

You, even you, are Lord alone;
You have made heaven,

The heaven of heavens,
With all their host,

The earth,
And all things that are therein,

The seas,
And all that is therein,

And you preserve them all;
And the host of heaven worships you.

A History of Rebellion and Grace

You chose Abram and called him Abraham.
You gave the land to his seed,

And you performed your words;
For you are righteous.

You saw the affliction of our fathers in Egypt,
And divided the sea before your people.

You led them by day by a cloudy pillar;
And in the night by a pillar of fire,

To give them light
In the way wherein they should go.

You gave them your laws, and manna, and water.
And promised them that they should go in to possess the land.

But our stubborn fathers acted arrogantly,
Neither were mindful of the wonders you did among them,

But stubbornly, in their rebellion, appointed a captain
To return to their bondage.

But you are a God
  Ready to pardon,
  Gracious and merciful,
  Slow to anger,
  And of great kindness,
And did not forsake them.

Indeed, even when they made the calf idol,

Even then, in your great compassion,

You did not abandon them in the wilderness,
But continued to lead them in the way.

Truly, forty years you did sustain them in the wilderness.
In all that time they lacked nothing.

Their clothes did not wear out,
And their feet did not swell.

And then you gave them kingdoms and nations,
And divided the land so all had their own places.

And they took over houses full of good things;
So they did eat, and were filled, and became fat,

And delighted themselves
In your great goodness.

Nevertheless, they were disobedient, and rebelled against you.
And so you delivered them into the hand of their enemies.

And in the time of their trouble, when they cried unto you,
In your compassion, you delivered them . . . time after time.

When a man keeps your Law,
He shall live.

A Plea

Now, therefore, our God,
    The great,
    The mighty,
    And the awe-inspiring God,
Who keeps his gracious covenant,

Do not let all the trouble seem trifling to you
That has come upon us,
    On our kings,
    On our princes,
    On our priests,
    On our prophets,
    On our fathers,
    On all thy people,
Since the time of the kings of Assyria unto this day.

You have always been righteous in your judgments,
For you have acted faithfully, but we have acted wickedly.

Neither have
    Our kings,
    Our princes,
    Our priests,
    Nor our fathers,
Kept your Law,

Nor listened to the commandments and warnings
You gave them.

Even when they were in their kingdom,
The one you gave them in your great goodness,

In the spacious and fertile land you gave them,
They did not serve you, nor turn away from their wicked works.

And so we are slaves today in the land you gave our fathers.
Where we should eat the fruit and the good of the land,

Instead, we are slaves.
And the abundant harvest goes to the kings

Who you set over us because of our sins.
They rule over us and our animals.

We are in great distress.

And because of all this,
We are making a firm covenant,

And putting it in writing,
Sealing it with the names of
        Our princes,
        And Levites,
        And priests.

Sealed

The list of the sealed
Begins with
Nehemiah,

Called the Tirshatha,
The governor,
The son of Hachaliah,

And continues with another
Seventy-nine names,
Eighty in all,

The chiefs of the priests,
The chiefs of the Levites,
The chiefs of the people.

An Oath

The rest of the people:
  The priests,
  The Levites,
  The gatekeepers,
  The singers,
  The Nethinim,
And all who had separated themselves
From the people of the lands
Unto the law of God,

With their wives,
  Their sons,
  And their daughters,
All able to have knowledge and understanding—

They joined with their brothers, the nobles,
And took an oath, swearing a curse on themselves if they failed,

To walk in God's law,
Which was given by Moses the servant of God,

And to observe and do
All the commandments of the Lord our Lord,
  And his regulations
  And his decrees.

Agreed Together

We will not give our daughters to the people of the land,
Nor take their daughters for our sons.

And if the people of the land seek to sell goods or grain
On the Sabbath, we will not buy.

We will let the fields lie fallow every seventh year,
And cancel every debt.

We will pay the annual tax
For all the work of the house of our God.

We will cast lots to bring the wood offering
      into the house of our God,
At the proper time, as is written in the law.

And we will bring the firstfruits
Year by year, to the house of the Lord.

We will not forsake the house of our God.

Dwelling

And the rulers of the people dwelt at Jerusalem.

The rest of the people cast lots,
So one in ten came to live in Jerusalem the holy city,
While the other nine in ten dwelt in other cities.

And the people blessed all the men who volunteered
To dwell in Jerusalem.

Critical Mass

The success of a city depends,
In part,
On having enough residents
To maintain and trade and manage.

If the capital city lies deserted,
What does it matter if the wall protects?

Dedication

403 B.C.
At the dedication of the wall of Jerusalem,
All the Levites assembled in Jerusalem
To keep the dedication with gladness,
>Both with thanksgivings,
>And with singing,
>With cymbals, harps, and lyres.

And the sons of the singers gathered themselves together,
From the villages they had built for themselves around Jerusalem.

And the priests and the Levites
>Purified themselves,
>And purified the people,
>And the gates,
>And the wall.

Then I brought up the princes of Judah upon the wall,
And appointed two great choirs that gave thanks:

One to the south upon the wall toward the Dung Gate,
Along with certain of the priests' sons with trumpets,
And with the musical instruments of David the man of God,
And Ezra the scribe went before them.

At the Fountain Gate they went up the stairs of the city of David,
On the ascent of the wall,
And passed above the site of David's palace,
To the Water Gate on the east.

The other choir of thanksgiving went to the north.
I followed after them,
With the half of the people upon the wall.

We went until we met,
And the two companies
Gave thanks in the house of God.

And the singers sang loudly.

Also that day they offered great sacrifices, and rejoiced:
For God had made them rejoice with great joy.

The wives also and the children rejoiced:
So that the joy of Jerusalem was heard even

Afar off.

Appointed

At that time some were appointed
Over the storerooms for the treasures,
    For the offerings,
    For the firstfruits,
    And for the tithes,
To gather the portions required by Law
For the priests and Levites
From the fields outside the towns.

For all Judah rejoiced
In the priests and the Levites and their work,
For they performed the service of their God,
And the service of purification,
As did the singers and the gatekeepers,

According to the commandment of David,
And of Solomon his son.

Singers

For long ago in the days of David
And Asaph the worship director,

There were directors of the singers,
And songs of praise and thanksgiving unto God.

And now, in the days of Zerubbabel and Nehemiah,
All Israel contributed daily portions
To the singers and the gatekeepers.

And they set apart the portion for the Levites;
And the Levites set apart the portion for the priests,
The descendants of Aaron.

A New Revelation

On that day,
As they read the book of Moses
In the company of the people,
They read that the men of Ammon
       And the men of Moab
Should not come into the congregation of God
For ever,

Because they had not met the children of Israel
With bread and with water.

Rather, Balak hired Balaam to curse them,
Though God turned the curse into a blessing.

Separation

So it came to pass,
When they had heard the law,
That they separated from Israel
All those of mixed ancestry.

Separated.

A single sentence in the telling,
Easy words to pass over,

Masking the hard reality
    Of legal proceedings,
    Of torn relationships,
    Of heartache.

Rebellion in the Ranks

In the Interim

Eliashib the priest, appointed as overseer
Of the storehouses of the house of our God,
Was allied by marriage to Tobiah the Ammonite,
My nemesis of old.

The priest had prepared for Tobiah a large room,
Where the people used to store
    The meat offerings,
    The frankincense,
    The vessels,
    The tithes of grain,
    The new wine,
    And the oil,

Which was commanded to be given to
    The Levites,
    And the singers,
    And the gatekeepers;
    And the offerings of the priests.

A large room indeed,
In the Temple itself,
Where Ammonites were not to go,
Let alone to live.

Purification

When I came to Jerusalem,
And understood the evil that Eliashib did for Tobiah,
In preparing him a chamber in the courts of the house of God,

I was sorely grieved, greatly displeased,
And I threw all of the household stuff of Tobiah
Out of the chamber.

Then I ordered that the rooms be purified,
And I brought back the vessels of the house of God,
    With the meat offering
    And the frankincense.

More Bad Tidings

And I realized that the portions assigned to the Levites
Had not been given them,

For the Levites and the singers that did the work
Had returned to their fields. They needed to eat!

So much for the oath of the people
That they would bring the firstfruits.

So much for the oath of the people
That they would not neglect the house of God.

Correction

So I rebuked the rulers, and said,
"Why is the house of God forsaken?"

Then I assembled the Levites and singers,
And stationed them at their posts.

Then all Judah brought the tithe of grain
     And the new wine
     And the oil unto the treasuries.

And I set four faithful men in charge of the treasuries:
A priest, a scribe, a Levite, and an assistant.
Their job was to distribute the supplies to their brethren.

Remember Me

Remember me for this,
O my God,
And do not wipe my good deeds
That I have done for the house of my God,
And for its services.

Should Not Be Done

In those days, I saw in Judah
Some treading wine presses on the Sabbath,
  And bringing in sheaves,
  And loading donkeys with burden;
  As also wine, grapes, figs, and all manner of burdens,
Which they brought into Jerusalem on the Sabbath day.
I testified against them about selling food on that day.

Also men of neighboring Tyre lived in Jerusalem
And imported fish and all kinds of goods,
And sold these on the Sabbath to the children of Judah,
  And in Jerusalem.

So much for the oath of the people
That they would not buy or sell on the Sabbath day.

Rebuke

Then I rebuked the nobles of Judah,
And said unto them,
"What evil thing is this that you do,
Profaning the Sabbath day?

Don't you remember?
This is what your fathers did,
And as a result, our God brought all this evil upon us,
        And upon this city!

Yet you intend to bring more wrath upon Israel
By profaning the Sabbath."

Plan

And it came to pass,
That when the evening shadows
Reached the gates of Jerusalem
Before the Sabbath,

I commanded that the gates should be shut,
And charged that they should not be opened
Till after the Sabbath.

I set some of my trustworthy servants at the gates,
That there should no burden be brought in on the Sabbath day.

Camping

The merchants camped outside Jerusalem
Once or twice.

Then I warned them, and said to them,
"Why are you camping outside the wall?
If you do so again, I will arrest you."

From that time on,
They came no more on the Sabbath.

Purification

I also commanded the Levites
That they should purify themselves,
And that they should come and keep the gates,
To keep the Sabbath day holy.

Prayer

Remember me,
O my God,
Concerning this also,
And spare me
According to the greatness
Of thy mercy.

Intermarriage

In those days also, I saw Jews
That had married wives of Ashdod,
      Of Ammon,
      And of Moab.

Their children spoke the language of Ashdod,
Or one of the other peoples,
But could not speak in the Jews' language.

So much for the oath of the people
That they would not intermarry with the surrounding peoples.

Punishment

And I rebuked them,
And cursed them.

Their disobedience put all at risk!

Some I had beaten,
And some had their hair pulled out.

I made them swear by God,
Repeating after me:
"You shall not give your daughters to their sons,
Nor take their daughters to your sons,
      Or for yourselves."

Did not Solomon king of Israel sin by these things?
Among the many nations, there was no king like him,
Who was beloved of his God,
And God made him king over all Israel.
Nevertheless, even he was led into sin by his foreign wives.

Why should we hear that you, too,
Do all this great evil,
Sinning against our God in marrying foreign women?

Sanballat Again

One of the grandsons of Eliashib the high priest
Was son-in-law to Sanballat the Horonite.
I banished him.

Words or Actions

Though with words my people may praise God,
They find it hard to follow through with action.

A dedicated and purified Temple
Is a monument of God's faithfulness,

But our treatment of that Temple
Is a reminder of our faithlessness.

A dedicated and completed wall
Is a monument of God's faithfulness,

But no wall is enough to keep out
Willful disobedience.

Perhaps one day we shall have
A better Temple, a better Protector.

Prayer

Remember them,
O my God,
Because they have defiled the priesthood,
    And the covenant of the priesthood,
    And of the Levites.

Thus cleansed I them from all strangers,
And assigned the duties of the priests and the Levites,
Every one in his business.

And I arranged for contributions for the wood offering,
At appointed times,
And for the firstfruits.

Remember me,
O my God,
For good.

Epilogue

Later

Though that is the end of the book of Nehemiah,
And the last of the Old Testament histories—
Chronologically, that is
(No other record after 403 B.C.)—
The Apocrypha gives an additional statement:

Nehemiah, "founding a library,
Gathered together the books
About the kings and the prophets,
And the books of David,
And letters of kings about sacred gifts."

We might call this effort Chronicles.

Author's Note

On Kingly Names and Titles

From *The Companion Bible:* "The names of some of the kings mentioned have been hitherto regarded as proper names; whereas, according to Sir Henry Rawlinson, Professor Sayce, T*he Encyclopedia Britannica*, and *The Century Encyclopedia of Names*, three at least are appellatives (like Pharaoh, Abimelech, Czar, Shah, Sultan); viz. Ahasuerus, which means 'The venerable king', Artaxerxes, which means 'The great king', and Darius, which means 'The maintainer'. . . . If these appellatives denote separate and different individual kings, no place can be found for them all on the page of history."

Did you catch that? "Artaxerxes" is not a proper name, like "George Washington," but a title, like "President." This helps resolve chronological differences.

Imagine how challenging history would be if, in almost three thousand years, historians tried to make sense of the history of the United States and kept coming across fragmentary mentions of "President." This person apparently fought in war after war, and did an astonishing number of things.

But, like dozens of presidents, Babylon had multiple kings.

The Companion Bible lists these kings, from the start of Nehemiah to the end:

461-454 B.C. Nebuchadnezzar's seven years of madness
454 Twentieth year of Asteiages (Artaxerxes).
452 Nebuchadnezzar dies after 44 years' reign
452 Evil-Merodach
446 Nabouidus
429 Belshazzar, 3 years

426 Belshazzar slain. "Darius the Median" (Asteiages) takes the kingdom
426 Cyrus (Asteiages' son) issues the Decree to rebuild the Temple
421 Cyrus ends
418 Cambyses makes Nehemiah governor
411 Darius Hystaspis re-enacts the decrees of Cyrus

What a tumultuous time in history!

On Dates and Controversies

Historians debate: were Ezra and Nehemiah contemporaries? Or was Ezra a generation before? Most modern scholarship places Ezra many decades before Nehemiah.

Coming back to that in a moment—some years ago, I read Dr. Peter Leithart's outstanding study on I and II Samuel, *A House for My Name*. He talked about how the ancient historians were not as tied to chronology as we are today. The writers might put certain events at the beginning or the end for emphasis. Thus, II Samuel ends with David buying a threshing floor, an event that had happened far earlier in his life. So why did the author put it there? Because the threshing floor is the place where the Temple would be built. If I remember correctly, this creates a bookend to the Samuels: starting with the Tabernacle in neglect, and ending with looking ahead to the building of the Temple.

Artistically, this is lovely. But for readers in the present-day, who are used to following the cause and effect of events, the method of organizing events in order to increase emphasis is confusing. It looks almost sloppy.

With this in mind, I have chosen to follow, as best as I can, the chronology given in *The Companion Bible*. The note-compilers make the case that Nehemiah and Ezra were contemporaries, and that the events of the two books intertwine.

Chronologically, Nehemiah is the beginning. After all, Jerusalem would hardly have been almost abandoned and desolate if the 42,360 exiles who returned with Ezra had recently arrived.

But in the Scriptures Ezra comes first because, to the Jews, Ezra's emphasis on the Temple takes precedence over Nehemiah's emphasis on the wall.

So Nehemiah begins chronologically, and when the wall is finished, "the houses were not yet builded," and when the Feast of Booths was kept, "the foundation of the Temple of the Lord was not yet laid" (Ezra 3:1-6).

We know from Haggai that the people had rebuilt their houses before they finished rebuilding the Temple.

There are certain definite ties between Ezra and Nehemiah, where the two books describe the same event. Those are anchoring points to help make sense of the chronology.

I was surprised, at the end, to see how well the story flowed, when I used the chronology in *The Companion Bible*.

Any errors, of course, are my own.

Benediction

May you go forward, like Nehemiah, in faithfulness and prayer, as you serve a merciful and gracious God.